50 Lazy Chef's Guide to Easy Meals

By: Kelly Johnson

Table of Contents

- One-Pan Lemon Garlic Chicken
- 5-Ingredient Beef Tacos
- Easy Veggie Stir-Fry
- Sheet Pan Sausage and Veggies
- Quick Tomato Basil Pasta
- 3-Ingredient BBQ Chicken
- Simple Fried Rice
- Microwave Mug Omelette
- Instant Pot Chili
- No-Cook Greek Salad
- Easy Quesadillas
- 15-Minute Shrimp Scampi
- Canned Tuna Pasta Salad
- Overnight Oats
- Simple Baked Salmon
- Rotisserie Chicken Tacos
- One-Pot Cheesy Broccoli Rice
- Easy Caprese Salad
- 5-Minute Hummus Wrap
- Quick Vegetable Soup
- Instant Pot Mac and Cheese
- No-Bake Peanut Butter Bars
- Quick Pesto Pasta
- Simple Avocado Toast
- One-Skillet Breakfast Hash
- 3-Ingredient Pancakes
- Easy Baked Potatoes
- Slow Cooker Beef Stew
- Simple Chicken Caesar Salad
- Frozen Veggie Stir-Fry
- Canned Bean Salad
- 4-Ingredient Chili
- Easy Veggie Frittata
- One-Pan Chicken and Rice
- Quick Tomato Soup

- 5-Minute Guacamole
- Easy Baked Ziti
- One-Pot Lemon Orzo
- Quick Corn and Black Bean Salad
- Easy Egg Fried Rice
- Simple Pita Pizzas
- No-Cook Pasta Salad
- 5-Ingredient Sloppy Joes
- Easy Chicken Noodle Soup
- Quick Veggie Tacos
- Instant Pot Beef Stroganoff
- One-Pan Fajitas
- 3-Ingredient Fruit Salad
- Easy Spaghetti Aglio e Olio
- Canned Soup Casserole

One-Pan Lemon Garlic Chicken

Ingredients:

- **For the chicken:**
    - 4 boneless, skinless chicken breasts
    - 1 tablespoon olive oil
    - Salt and pepper, to taste
    - 1 teaspoon paprika
    - 1 teaspoon dried oregano
    - 4 cloves garlic, minced
    - Zest and juice of 1 lemon
- **For the vegetables:**
    - 2 cups baby potatoes, halved
    - 1 cup green beans, trimmed
    - 1 tablespoon butter
    - Fresh parsley, chopped (for garnish)

Instructions:

1. **Preheat the Oven:** Preheat your oven to 400°F (200°C).
2. **Prepare the Chicken:** In a large bowl, combine olive oil, salt, pepper, paprika, oregano, minced garlic, lemon zest, and lemon juice. Add the chicken breasts and coat them well in the marinade. Let them marinate for at least 15 minutes (or up to 2 hours in the fridge for more flavor).
3. **Prepare the Vegetables:** In a large oven-safe skillet or baking dish, arrange the halved baby potatoes. Drizzle with olive oil, salt, and pepper. Toss to coat. Place in the preheated oven and roast for about 20 minutes.
4. **Add Chicken and Green Beans:** After 20 minutes, remove the skillet from the oven. Push the potatoes to one side and place the marinated chicken breasts in the center. Add the green beans around the chicken and potatoes. Dot the butter on top of the chicken.
5. **Bake:** Return the skillet to the oven and bake for an additional 25-30 minutes, or until the chicken is cooked through (internal temperature of 165°F/75°C) and the vegetables are tender.
6. **Serve:** Remove from the oven and let it rest for a few minutes. Garnish with fresh parsley before serving.

5-Ingredient Beef Tacos

Ingredients:

- 1 lb ground beef
- 1 packet taco seasoning
- 8 small taco shells
- 1 cup shredded lettuce
- 1 cup diced tomatoes

Instructions:

1. **Cook the Beef:** In a skillet over medium heat, cook the ground beef until browned. Drain excess fat.
2. **Season:** Add the taco seasoning and follow package instructions (usually add water and simmer for a few minutes).
3. **Assemble Tacos:** Fill each taco shell with the seasoned beef, then top with shredded lettuce and diced tomatoes.
4. **Serve:** Enjoy immediately, or serve with your favorite taco toppings like cheese or salsa.

Easy Veggie Stir-Fry

Ingredients:

- 2 cups mixed vegetables (e.g., bell peppers, broccoli, carrots)
- 1 tablespoon soy sauce
- 1 tablespoon olive oil
- 2 cloves garlic, minced
- Cooked rice or noodles (for serving)

Instructions:

1. **Heat Oil:** In a large pan or wok, heat the olive oil over medium-high heat.
2. **Add Garlic:** Add minced garlic and sauté for 30 seconds until fragrant.
3. **Stir-Fry Veggies:** Add the mixed vegetables and stir-fry for about 5-7 minutes, until tender-crisp.
4. **Season:** Drizzle soy sauce over the veggies and stir to combine.
5. **Serve:** Serve over cooked rice or noodles.

Sheet Pan Sausage and Veggies

Ingredients:

- 1 lb smoked sausage (e.g., kielbasa), sliced
- 2 cups mixed vegetables (e.g., zucchini, bell peppers, onions)
- 2 tablespoons olive oil
- 1 teaspoon Italian seasoning
- Salt and pepper, to taste

Instructions:

1. **Preheat Oven:** Preheat your oven to 400°F (200°C).
2. **Prepare the Pan:** On a large sheet pan, combine the sliced sausage and mixed vegetables.
3. **Season:** Drizzle with olive oil, sprinkle with Italian seasoning, salt, and pepper. Toss to coat evenly.
4. **Bake:** Bake in the preheated oven for 25-30 minutes, or until the veggies are tender and the sausage is heated through.
5. **Serve:** Enjoy hot as a complete meal.

Quick Tomato Basil Pasta

Ingredients:

- 8 oz pasta (spaghetti or your choice)
- 2 cups cherry tomatoes, halved
- 2 cloves garlic, minced
- 1/4 cup fresh basil, chopped
- 2 tablespoons olive oil

Instructions:

1. **Cook Pasta:** Cook pasta according to package instructions. Reserve 1/2 cup of pasta water, then drain.
2. **Sauté Tomatoes:** In a large skillet, heat olive oil over medium heat. Add garlic and sauté for 1 minute, then add cherry tomatoes and cook until soft.
3. **Combine:** Toss the cooked pasta with the tomatoes, reserved pasta water, and fresh basil. Season with salt and pepper to taste.

3-Ingredient BBQ Chicken

Ingredients:

- 1 lb boneless chicken breasts
- 1 cup BBQ sauce
- 1 tablespoon olive oil

Instructions:

1. **Preheat Oven:** Preheat oven to 375°F (190°C).
2. **Prepare Chicken:** In a skillet, heat olive oil over medium heat. Sear chicken breasts on both sides until golden brown.
3. **Bake:** Place chicken in a baking dish, pour BBQ sauce over, and bake for 20-25 minutes until cooked through.

Simple Fried Rice

Ingredients:

- 2 cups cooked rice (preferably day-old)
- 1 cup mixed vegetables (frozen or fresh)
- 2 eggs, beaten
- 2 tablespoons soy sauce
- 1 tablespoon sesame oil (or vegetable oil)

Instructions:

1. **Heat Oil:** In a large skillet or wok, heat sesame oil over medium-high heat.
2. **Scramble Eggs:** Add beaten eggs and scramble until cooked. Remove and set aside.
3. **Fry Rice:** Add mixed vegetables and rice to the skillet, stir-fry for a few minutes, then add soy sauce and scrambled eggs. Mix well and serve.

Microwave Mug Omelette

Ingredients:

- 2 eggs
- 2 tablespoons milk
- 1/4 cup diced vegetables (e.g., bell peppers, onions)
- Salt and pepper, to taste
- Optional: shredded cheese

Instructions:

1. **Mix Ingredients:** In a microwave-safe mug, whisk together eggs, milk, diced vegetables, salt, and pepper.
2. **Microwave:** Microwave on high for 1 minute, stir, then microwave for an additional 30 seconds or until eggs are set.
3. **Serve:** Top with cheese if desired and enjoy.

Instant Pot Chili

Ingredients:

- 1 lb ground beef (or turkey)
- 1 can (15 oz) kidney beans, drained and rinsed
- 1 can (15 oz) diced tomatoes
- 1 packet chili seasoning
- 1 cup beef broth

Instructions:

1. **Sauté Meat:** Turn the Instant Pot to sauté mode. Add ground meat and cook until browned, then drain excess fat.
2. **Add Ingredients:** Stir in beans, tomatoes, chili seasoning, and beef broth.
3. **Pressure Cook:** Seal the lid, set to manual high pressure for 15 minutes, then allow to release naturally.

No-Cook Greek Salad

Ingredients:

- 1 cup cherry tomatoes, halved
- 1 cucumber, diced
- 1 cup Kalamata olives
- 1/2 cup feta cheese, crumbled
- 2 tablespoons olive oil

Instructions:

1. **Combine Ingredients:** In a large bowl, combine cherry tomatoes, cucumber, olives, and feta cheese.
2. **Dress Salad:** Drizzle with olive oil, season with salt and pepper, and toss gently. Serve immediately.

Easy Quesadillas

Ingredients:

- 4 flour tortillas
- 2 cups shredded cheese (cheddar, Monterey Jack, or your choice)
- 1 cup cooked chicken or beans (optional)
- Salsa (for serving)

Instructions:

1. **Assemble Quesadillas:** On half of each tortilla, layer cheese and optional chicken or beans. Fold over.
2. **Cook:** In a skillet over medium heat, cook quesadillas for 2-3 minutes on each side until golden brown and cheese is melted.
3. **Serve:** Cut into wedges and serve with salsa.

15-Minute Shrimp Scampi

Ingredients:

- 1 lb shrimp, peeled and deveined
- 4 cloves garlic, minced
- 1/4 cup butter
- 1/4 cup fresh parsley, chopped
- Juice of 1 lemon

Instructions:

1. **Sauté Garlic:** In a large skillet, melt butter over medium heat. Add garlic and sauté for 1 minute.
2. **Cook Shrimp:** Add shrimp and cook until pink, about 3-4 minutes.
3. **Finish Dish:** Stir in lemon juice and parsley. Serve immediately over pasta or rice.

Canned Tuna Pasta Salad

Ingredients:

- 8 oz pasta (rotini or shell)
- 1 can (15 oz) tuna, drained
- 1 cup cherry tomatoes, halved
- 1/2 cup mayonnaise
- 1 tablespoon lemon juice

Instructions:

1. **Cook Pasta:** Cook pasta according to package instructions. Drain and cool.
2. **Mix Ingredients:** In a large bowl, combine cooked pasta, tuna, cherry tomatoes, mayonnaise, and lemon juice.
3. **Serve:** Season with salt and pepper to taste, then serve chilled or at room temperature.

Overnight Oats

Ingredients:

- 1/2 cup rolled oats
- 1/2 cup milk (dairy or non-dairy)
- 1/2 cup yogurt (optional)
- 1 tablespoon honey or maple syrup
- Toppings of your choice (e.g., fruit, nuts, seeds)

Instructions:

1. **Combine Ingredients:** In a jar or bowl, mix oats, milk, yogurt, and sweetener.
2. **Refrigerate:** Cover and refrigerate overnight.
3. **Serve:** In the morning, stir and add your favorite toppings before enjoying.

Simple Baked Salmon

Ingredients:

- 4 salmon fillets
- 2 tablespoons olive oil
- Salt and pepper, to taste
- 1 lemon, sliced
- Fresh dill (optional)

Instructions:

1. **Preheat Oven:** Preheat oven to 400°F (200°C).
2. **Prepare Salmon:** Place salmon fillets on a baking sheet lined with parchment paper. Drizzle with olive oil, then season with salt and pepper. Top with lemon slices and dill if using.
3. **Bake:** Bake for 12-15 minutes or until salmon flakes easily with a fork.

Rotisserie Chicken Tacos

Ingredients:

- 2 cups rotisserie chicken, shredded
- 8 small taco shells
- 1 cup shredded lettuce
- 1/2 cup diced tomatoes
- 1/2 cup salsa

Instructions:

1. **Prepare Chicken:** Remove skin and bones from the rotisserie chicken and shred the meat.
2. **Assemble Tacos:** Fill each taco shell with shredded chicken, lettuce, and diced tomatoes.
3. **Serve:** Top with salsa and serve immediately.

One-Pot Cheesy Broccoli Rice

Ingredients:

- 1 cup rice (white or brown)
- 2 cups vegetable or chicken broth
- 2 cups broccoli florets
- 1 cup shredded cheese (cheddar or your choice)
- Salt and pepper, to taste

Instructions:

1. **Combine Ingredients:** In a large pot, combine rice and broth. Bring to a boil.
2. **Add Broccoli:** Stir in broccoli, cover, and reduce heat to low. Cook until rice is tender and liquid is absorbed, about 15-20 minutes.
3. **Add Cheese:** Remove from heat, stir in cheese, and season with salt and pepper. Serve warm.

Easy Caprese Salad

Ingredients:

- 2 large tomatoes, sliced
- 8 oz fresh mozzarella cheese, sliced
- Fresh basil leaves
- 2 tablespoons olive oil
- Balsamic vinegar (optional)

Instructions:

1. **Layer Ingredients:** On a serving platter, alternate layers of tomato slices, mozzarella slices, and basil leaves.
2. **Dress Salad:** Drizzle with olive oil and balsamic vinegar if desired. Season with salt and pepper to taste.
3. **Serve:** Enjoy immediately.

5-Minute Hummus Wrap

Ingredients:

- 1 large tortilla or wrap
- 1/2 cup hummus
- 1 cup mixed greens
- 1/2 cucumber, sliced
- 1/2 bell pepper, sliced

Instructions:

1. **Spread Hummus:** Spread hummus evenly over the tortilla.
2. **Add Veggies:** Layer mixed greens, cucumber, and bell pepper on top.
3. **Wrap and Serve:** Roll the tortilla tightly, slice in half, and serve.

Quick Vegetable Soup

Ingredients:

- 4 cups vegetable broth
- 2 cups mixed vegetables (fresh or frozen)
- 1 can (15 oz) diced tomatoes
- 1 teaspoon Italian seasoning
- Salt and pepper, to taste

Instructions:

1. **Combine Ingredients:** In a large pot, combine vegetable broth, mixed vegetables, diced tomatoes, and Italian seasoning.
2. **Cook:** Bring to a boil, then reduce heat and simmer for 15-20 minutes until vegetables are tender.
3. **Serve:** Season with salt and pepper, then enjoy hot.

Instant Pot Mac and Cheese

Ingredients:

- 8 oz elbow macaroni
- 1 cup water
- 1 tablespoon butter
- 2 cups shredded cheddar cheese
- Salt and pepper, to taste

Instructions:

1. **Combine Ingredients:** In the Instant Pot, combine macaroni, water, and butter.
2. **Pressure Cook:** Seal the lid and set to manual high pressure for 4 minutes. Once done, perform a quick release.
3. **Add Cheese:** Stir in shredded cheese and season with salt and pepper. Mix until creamy and serve.

No-Bake Peanut Butter Bars

Ingredients:

- 1 cup peanut butter
- 1 cup rolled oats
- 1/2 cup honey or maple syrup
- 1/2 cup chocolate chips (optional)
- 1/2 teaspoon vanilla extract

Instructions:

1. **Mix Ingredients:** In a bowl, combine peanut butter, oats, honey, and vanilla extract. Stir until well mixed.
2. **Add Chocolate:** If using, fold in chocolate chips.
3. **Set Bars:** Press the mixture into an 8x8-inch baking dish. Refrigerate for at least 1 hour, then cut into bars.

Quick Pesto Pasta

Ingredients:

- 8 oz pasta (your choice)
- 1/2 cup pesto sauce
- 1/4 cup grated Parmesan cheese
- Cherry tomatoes, halved (optional)
- Salt and pepper, to taste

Instructions:

1. **Cook Pasta:** Cook pasta according to package instructions. Drain and return to pot.
2. **Combine Ingredients:** Stir in pesto sauce and Parmesan cheese. Add cherry tomatoes if desired.
3. **Serve:** Season with salt and pepper, and serve warm.

Simple Avocado Toast

Ingredients:

- 1 ripe avocado
- 2 slices of bread (whole grain or your choice)
- Salt and pepper, to taste
- Optional toppings: cherry tomatoes, red pepper flakes, or a poached egg

Instructions:

1. **Toast Bread:** Toast the bread slices until golden brown.
2. **Prepare Avocado:** Mash the avocado in a bowl and season with salt and pepper.
3. **Assemble:** Spread the mashed avocado on the toasted bread and add optional toppings if desired. Serve immediately.

One-Skillet Breakfast Hash

Ingredients:

- 2 cups diced potatoes
- 1 bell pepper, diced
- 1 onion, diced
- 4 eggs
- Salt and pepper, to taste

Instructions:

1. **Cook Potatoes:** In a large skillet, cook diced potatoes over medium heat until tender and golden brown, about 10-12 minutes.
2. **Add Vegetables:** Stir in bell pepper and onion, cooking until softened.
3. **Add Eggs:** Make four wells in the hash and crack an egg into each. Cover and cook until eggs are set. Season with salt and pepper before serving.

3-Ingredient Pancakes

Ingredients:

- 1 ripe banana
- 2 eggs
- 1/2 teaspoon baking powder

Instructions:

1. **Mash Banana:** In a bowl, mash the banana until smooth.
2. **Combine Ingredients:** Whisk in eggs and baking powder until fully combined.
3. **Cook Pancakes:** Heat a non-stick skillet over medium heat and pour batter to form pancakes. Cook for 2-3 minutes on each side until golden brown.

Easy Baked Potatoes

Ingredients:

- 4 medium russet potatoes
- Olive oil
- Salt, to taste
- Optional toppings: butter, sour cream, cheese, chives

Instructions:

1. **Preheat Oven:** Preheat oven to 425°F (220°C).
2. **Prepare Potatoes:** Wash and poke holes in the potatoes. Rub with olive oil and sprinkle with salt.
3. **Bake:** Place potatoes directly on the oven rack and bake for 45-60 minutes until tender. Serve with your choice of toppings.

Slow Cooker Beef Stew

Ingredients:

- 1.5 lbs beef chuck, cut into cubes
- 4 cups beef broth
- 3 carrots, sliced
- 2 potatoes, diced
- 1 onion, chopped

Instructions:

1. **Combine Ingredients:** In a slow cooker, combine beef, broth, carrots, potatoes, and onion.
2. **Cook:** Cover and cook on low for 7-8 hours or on high for 4-5 hours until beef is tender.
3. **Serve:** Season with salt and pepper before serving.

Simple Chicken Caesar Salad

Ingredients:

- 2 cups cooked chicken, diced
- 4 cups romaine lettuce, chopped
- 1/2 cup Caesar dressing
- 1/4 cup grated Parmesan cheese
- Croutons, for topping

Instructions:

1. **Combine Ingredients:** In a large bowl, mix the diced chicken, romaine lettuce, and Caesar dressing.
2. **Add Cheese:** Toss in the grated Parmesan cheese and mix well.
3. **Serve:** Top with croutons and serve immediately.

Frozen Veggie Stir-Fry

Ingredients:

- 4 cups frozen mixed vegetables
- 2 tablespoons soy sauce
- 1 tablespoon olive oil
- 1 teaspoon garlic powder
- Cooked rice or noodles, for serving

Instructions:

1. **Heat Oil:** In a large skillet, heat olive oil over medium heat.
2. **Stir-Fry Veggies:** Add frozen mixed vegetables and garlic powder. Cook for 5-7 minutes, stirring occasionally until heated through.
3. **Add Sauce:** Stir in soy sauce and cook for another minute. Serve over cooked rice or noodles.

Canned Bean Salad

Ingredients:

- 1 can (15 oz) kidney beans, drained and rinsed
- 1 can (15 oz) black beans, drained and rinsed
- 1 cup corn (canned or frozen)
- 1/2 cup diced red onion
- 1/4 cup olive oil

Instructions:

1. **Combine Ingredients:** In a large bowl, mix kidney beans, black beans, corn, and red onion.
2. **Dress Salad:** Drizzle with olive oil and toss to combine.
3. **Serve:** Chill for 30 minutes before serving for flavors to meld.

4-Ingredient Chili

Ingredients:

- 1 lb ground beef (or turkey)
- 1 can (15 oz) diced tomatoes
- 1 can (15 oz) kidney beans, drained and rinsed
- 1 packet chili seasoning mix

Instructions:

1. **Cook Meat:** In a large pot, brown the ground beef over medium heat until fully cooked. Drain excess fat.
2. **Add Ingredients:** Stir in diced tomatoes, kidney beans, and chili seasoning.
3. **Simmer:** Let simmer for 15-20 minutes, then serve hot.

Easy Veggie Frittata

Ingredients:

- 6 eggs
- 1 cup mixed vegetables (fresh or frozen)
- 1/2 cup shredded cheese
- Salt and pepper, to taste

Instructions:

1. **Preheat Oven:** Preheat the oven to 350°F (175°C).
2. **Whisk Eggs:** In a bowl, whisk together eggs, salt, and pepper. Stir in mixed vegetables and cheese.
3. **Bake:** Pour the mixture into a greased oven-safe skillet and bake for 20-25 minutes, or until set. Slice and serve.

One-Pan Chicken and Rice

Ingredients:

- 1 lb chicken thighs or breasts
- 1 cup rice (white or brown)
- 2 cups chicken broth
- 1 cup frozen peas and carrots
- Salt and pepper, to taste

Instructions:

1. **Sear Chicken:** In a large skillet, heat oil over medium heat. Season chicken with salt and pepper, then sear for 4-5 minutes on each side.
2. **Add Rice and Broth:** Stir in rice, chicken broth, and frozen peas and carrots. Bring to a boil.
3. **Cook:** Reduce heat, cover, and simmer for 20-25 minutes until rice is cooked and chicken is done. Fluff with a fork before serving.

Quick Tomato Soup

Ingredients:

- 1 can (28 oz) crushed tomatoes
- 2 cups vegetable or chicken broth
- 1 onion, chopped
- 1 tablespoon olive oil

Instructions:

1. **Sauté Onion:** In a pot, heat olive oil over medium heat. Add chopped onion and sauté until softened.
2. **Add Tomatoes and Broth:** Stir in crushed tomatoes and broth. Bring to a boil, then reduce heat and simmer for 10 minutes.
3. **Blend:** Use an immersion blender to blend until smooth. Season with salt and pepper, then serve.

5-Minute Guacamole

Ingredients:

- 2 ripe avocados
- 1 lime, juiced
- 1/2 teaspoon garlic powder
- Salt, to taste

Instructions:

1. **Mash Avocados:** In a bowl, mash the avocados with a fork.
2. **Add Ingredients:** Stir in lime juice, garlic powder, and salt.
3. **Serve:** Enjoy immediately with tortilla chips or as a topping.

Easy Baked Ziti

Ingredients:

- 1 lb ziti pasta
- 2 cups marinara sauce
- 2 cups ricotta cheese
- 2 cups shredded mozzarella cheese
- 1/2 cup grated Parmesan cheese

Instructions:

1. **Preheat Oven:** Preheat oven to 375°F (190°C).
2. **Cook Pasta:** Cook ziti according to package instructions until al dente. Drain and return to pot.
3. **Combine Ingredients:** Mix in marinara sauce, ricotta cheese, and half of the mozzarella. Transfer to a baking dish and top with remaining mozzarella and Parmesan.
4. **Bake:** Bake for 25-30 minutes until bubbly and golden. Serve warm.

One-Pot Lemon Orzo

Ingredients:

- 1 cup orzo pasta
- 4 cups vegetable broth
- 1 lemon, juiced and zested
- 1 cup spinach, chopped
- Salt and pepper, to taste

Instructions:

1. **Combine Ingredients:** In a pot, combine orzo, vegetable broth, lemon juice, and lemon zest.
2. **Cook:** Bring to a boil, then reduce heat and simmer for 10-12 minutes until orzo is tender.
3. **Add Spinach:** Stir in spinach and season with salt and pepper. Serve warm.

Quick Corn and Black Bean Salad

Ingredients:

- 1 can (15 oz) corn, drained
- 1 can (15 oz) black beans, drained and rinsed
- 1 bell pepper, diced
- 1/4 cup cilantro, chopped
- 2 tablespoons lime juice

Instructions:

1. **Combine Ingredients:** In a large bowl, mix corn, black beans, bell pepper, and cilantro.
2. **Dress Salad:** Drizzle with lime juice and toss to combine.
3. **Serve:** Chill for 15 minutes before serving to enhance flavors.

Easy Egg Fried Rice

Ingredients:

- 2 cups cooked rice (preferably day-old)
- 2 eggs, beaten
- 1 cup mixed vegetables (frozen or fresh)
- 2 tablespoons soy sauce
- 2 tablespoons green onions, chopped

Instructions:

1. **Scramble Eggs:** In a large skillet, scramble beaten eggs until fully cooked. Remove and set aside.
2. **Stir-Fry Rice:** In the same skillet, add mixed vegetables and cooked rice. Stir-fry for 5 minutes.
3. **Combine:** Stir in soy sauce, scrambled eggs, and green onions. Cook for another 2 minutes before serving.

Simple Pita Pizzas

Ingredients:

- 4 pita breads
- 1 cup marinara sauce
- 1 cup shredded mozzarella cheese
- 1/2 cup sliced pepperoni or other toppings of choice
- Italian seasoning, to taste

Instructions:

1. **Preheat Oven:** Preheat oven to 400°F (200°C).
2. **Assemble Pizzas:** Place pita breads on a baking sheet. Spread marinara sauce over each, top with mozzarella cheese and desired toppings.
3. **Bake:** Bake for 10-12 minutes until cheese is melted and bubbly. Serve warm.

No-Cook Pasta Salad

Ingredients:

- 8 oz cooked pasta (your choice)
- 1 cup cherry tomatoes, halved
- 1/2 cup mozzarella balls
- 1/4 cup olives, sliced
- 1/4 cup Italian dressing

Instructions:

1. **Combine Ingredients:** In a large bowl, mix cooked pasta, cherry tomatoes, mozzarella balls, and olives.
2. **Dress Salad:** Drizzle with Italian dressing and toss to combine.
3. **Serve:** Chill for 15 minutes before serving for best flavor.

5-Ingredient Sloppy Joes

Ingredients:

- 1 lb ground beef (or turkey)
- 1/2 cup ketchup
- 1/4 cup barbecue sauce
- 1 tablespoon Worcestershire sauce
- Hamburger buns

Instructions:

1. **Cook Meat:** In a skillet, cook ground beef over medium heat until browned. Drain excess fat.
2. **Add Sauce:** Stir in ketchup, barbecue sauce, and Worcestershire sauce. Simmer for 5 minutes.
3. **Serve:** Spoon mixture onto hamburger buns and serve immediately.

Easy Chicken Noodle Soup

Ingredients:

- 2 cups cooked chicken, shredded
- 4 cups chicken broth
- 2 cups egg noodles
- 1 cup carrots, sliced
- 1 cup celery, diced

Instructions:

1. **Combine Ingredients:** In a large pot, combine chicken broth, carrots, celery, and egg noodles.
2. **Cook Soup:** Bring to a boil, then reduce heat and simmer for 10 minutes until noodles are tender.
3. **Add Chicken:** Stir in shredded chicken and heat through. Serve hot.

Quick Veggie Tacos

Ingredients:

- 1 can (15 oz) black beans, drained and rinsed
- 1 cup corn (canned or frozen)
- 1 teaspoon cumin
- 8 small tortillas
- Toppings (e.g., avocado, salsa, cheese)

Instructions:

1. **Combine Ingredients:** In a bowl, mix black beans, corn, and cumin.
2. **Warm Tortillas:** Heat tortillas in a skillet or microwave until warm.
3. **Assemble Tacos:** Spoon veggie mixture onto tortillas and add desired toppings. Serve immediately.

Instant Pot Beef Stroganoff

Ingredients:

- 1 lb beef stew meat
- 1 onion, chopped
- 2 cups beef broth
- 1 cup mushrooms, sliced
- 1 cup sour cream

Instructions:

1. **Sauté Beef and Onion:** Set Instant Pot to sauté mode. Add beef and onion, cooking until beef is browned.
2. **Add Broth and Mushrooms:** Stir in beef broth and mushrooms. Close lid and cook on high pressure for 20 minutes.
3. **Finish with Sour Cream:** Quick release the pressure. Stir in sour cream and serve over egg noodles or rice.

One-Pan Fajitas

Ingredients:

- 1 lb chicken breast, sliced
- 1 bell pepper, sliced
- 1 onion, sliced
- 2 tablespoons fajita seasoning
- Tortillas, for serving

Instructions:

1. **Combine Ingredients:** In a large skillet, combine chicken, bell pepper, onion, and fajita seasoning.
2. **Cook:** Cook over medium heat for 10-12 minutes, stirring occasionally, until chicken is cooked through and veggies are tender.
3. **Serve:** Serve with warm tortillas.

3-Ingredient Fruit Salad

Ingredients:

- 2 cups mixed fresh fruit (e.g., berries, melons, grapes)
- 1/2 cup yogurt (plain or flavored)
- 1 tablespoon honey

Instructions:

1. **Combine Fruit:** In a large bowl, mix the fresh fruit.
2. **Add Dressing:** In a small bowl, whisk together yogurt and honey.
3. **Serve:** Drizzle yogurt mixture over the fruit salad and toss gently before serving.

Easy Spaghetti Aglio e Olio

Ingredients:

- 8 oz spaghetti
- 4 cloves garlic, thinly sliced
- 1/2 cup olive oil
- 1/4 teaspoon red pepper flakes
- Fresh parsley, chopped (for garnish)

Instructions:

1. **Cook Spaghetti:** Cook spaghetti according to package instructions until al dente. Reserve 1/2 cup pasta water and drain the rest.
2. **Sauté Garlic:** In a large skillet, heat olive oil over medium heat. Add garlic and red pepper flakes, cooking until garlic is golden.
3. **Combine:** Add cooked spaghetti and reserved pasta water to the skillet. Toss to coat. Garnish with parsley and serve.

Canned Soup Casserole

Ingredients:

- 2 cans (10.5 oz each) cream of chicken soup
- 1 cup cooked chicken, shredded
- 2 cups frozen mixed vegetables
- 2 cups cooked rice
- 1 cup shredded cheese

Instructions:

1. **Preheat Oven:** Preheat oven to 350°F (175°C).
2. **Combine Ingredients:** In a large bowl, mix cream of chicken soup, shredded chicken, frozen vegetables, and cooked rice.
3. **Transfer to Baking Dish:** Pour the mixture into a greased casserole dish and top with shredded cheese.
4. **Bake:** Bake for 25-30 minutes until heated through and cheese is bubbly. Serve warm.

www.ingramcontent.com/pod-product-compliance
Lightning Source LLC
LaVergne TN
LVHW061955070526
838199LV00060B/4136